Editor

Sara Connolly

Managing Editor

Ina Massler Levin, M.A.

Illustrator

Sue Fullam

Cover Artist

Brenda DiAntonis

Art Manager

Kevin Barnes

Art Director

CJae Froshay

Imaging

Craig Gunnell

Publisher

Mary D. Smith, M.S. Ed.

ASSESS
In One Page or Less

Grades 6-8

WITHDRAWN

Authors

Cynthia Gunderson

Suzanne Scotten

Teacher Created Resources, Inc.

6421 Industry Way

Westminster, CA 92683

www.teachercreated.com

ISBN-1-4206-3117-9

©2005 Teacher Created Resources, Inc.

Made in U.S.A.

Table of Contents

Introduction

Basic Paragraph Assessments

Quarter-page Assessments

Third-of-a-page Assessments

Half-page Assessments

Whole-page Assessments

Table of Contents (cont.)

Overview

The single-sheet assessment tools found in this book address a wide variety of standards, enabling teachers to have quick and easy samples to hold students accountable for information and skills presented in class. Specifically, the purpose is to enhance reading comprehension and increase writing opportunities in every classroom without creating an excessive grading burden on the teacher. In addition to serving as assessment tools, the activities can be used to reinforce literary devices, improve vocabulary and grammar skills, as well as develop concept understanding in any content area.

Assess in One Page or Less provides a variety of lessons and templates that can be incorporated into any content area lesson plan. The easy-to-use formats allow teachers to quickly and immediately assess a student's grasp of a concept, as well as provide accountability for comprehending a specific standard or objective. The adaptable activities promote incorporation of reading analysis, comprehension abilities, and summarization tools, as well as provide opportunities to increase and improve writing skills. The completed colorful products can then be used for bulletin boards, portfolios, performance assessments, or even mailed home to parents.

Although many of the ideas are listed as fitting on a quarter page, a third of a page, half page, or a whole page, once you become familiar with the concepts, you can easily reduce, enlarge, or adapt them to meet the needs of your classroom or content area. Some of the templates work better when duplicated onto heavier, cardstock paper.

To help ease your planning during this age of accountability, language arts standards are described and provided for each activity. In many schools, administrators require that objectives and standards be visibly posted for each lesson, and that these objectives are discussed with the students before the lesson, and assessed after each lesson. The one-page-or-less formats make it easy for teachers to satisfy these requirements without the burden of excessive paperwork.

Standards for Language Arts
Writing and Reading

Shown in the chart on page 9 are the standards for language arts that may be covered for each activity. Many of the lessons can incorporate more than one standard, depending on how you use the activity or template. The purpose of the chart is to help teachers easily identify potential activities for a standard or skill without searching through the whole book.

All states have their own standards, however most share some common elements and requirements. This chart references the universal collection of standards synthesized by John S. Kendall and Robert J. Marzano in their book *Content Knowledge: A Compendium of Standards and Benchmarks for K-12 Education* (Second Edition, 1997). This book is published jointly by McRel (Mid-continent Regional Educational Laboratory, Inc.) and ASCD (Association for Supervision and Curriculum Development). (Used by permission of McRel.) Specific descriptions of each standard follows.

Writing Standards – Level III (Grades 6-8)

1. **Demonstrates competence in the general skills and strategies of the writing process.**

   A. Prewriting: Uses a variety of prewriting strategies (e.g., makes outlines, uses published pieces as writing models, constructs critical standards, brainstorms, building background knowledge)

   B. Writes biographical sketches (e.g., illustrates the subject's character using narrative and descriptive strategies such as relevant dialogue, specific action, physical description, background description, and comparison or contrast to other people; reveals the significance of the subject to the writer; presents details in a logical manner)

   C. Writes in response to literature (e.g., anticipates and answers a reader's questions, responds to significant issues in a log or journal, answers discussion questions, writes a summary of a book, describes an initial impression of a text, connects knowledge from a text with personal knowledge.

2. **Demonstrates competence in the stylistic and rhetorical aspects of writing**

   A. Uses descriptive language that clarifies and enhances ideas (e.g., establishes tone and mood, uses figurative language)

   B. Uses paragraph form in writing (e.g., arranges sentences in sequential order, uses supporting and follow-up sentences)

3. **Uses grammatical and mechanical conventions in written compositions**

   A. Uses nouns in written compositions (e.g., forms possessives of nouns; forms irregular plural nouns)

Standards for Language Arts
Writing and Reading (cont.)

B. Uses verbs in written compositions (e.g., uses linking and auxiliary verbs, verb phrases, and correct forms of regular and irregular verbs)

C. Uses adjectives in written compositions (e.g., pronominal, positive, comparative, superlative)

D. Uses adverbs in written compositions (e.g., chooses between forms of adjectives and adverbs)

E. Uses prepositions and coordinating conjunctions in written compositions (e.g., uses prepositional phrases, combines and embeds ideas using conjunctions)

F. Uses conventions of capitalization in written compositions (e.g., titles, [books, stories, poems, magazines, newspapers, songs, words of art], proper nouns [team names, companies, schools and institutions, departments of government, religions, school subjects], proper adjectives, nationalities, brand names of products)

G. Uses conventions of punctuation in written compositions (e.g., uses exclamation marks after exclamatory sentences and interjections; uses periods in decimals, dollars, and cents; uses commas with nouns of address and after mild interjections; uses quotation marks with poems, songs, and chapters; uses colons in business letter salutations; uses hyphens to divide words between syllables at the end of a line)

4. **Gathers and uses information for research purposes**

A. Organizes information and ideas from multiple sources in systematic ways (e.g. time lines, outlines, notes, graphic representations)

Reading Standards—Level III (Grades 6-8)

5. **Demonstrates competence in the general skills and strategies of the reading process**

A. Generates interesting questions to be answered while reading

B. Establishes and adjusts purposes for reading (e.g., to understand, interpret, enjoy, solve problems, predict outcomes, answer a specific question, form an opinion, skim for facts)

C. Represents abstract information (e.g., concepts, generalizations) as explicit mental pictures

Standards for Language Arts
Writing and Reading (cont.)

D. Uses a variety of strategies to define and extend understanding of word meaning (e.g., applies knowledge of word origins and derivations, analogies, idioms, similes, metaphors)

E. Identifies specific devices an author uses to accomplish his or her purpose (e.g., persuasive techniques, style, literary form)

F. Reflects on what has been learned after reading and formulates ideas, opinions, and personal responses to texts

6. Demonstrates competence in the general skills and strategies for reading a variety of literary texts

A. Applies reading skills and strategies to a variety of literary passages and texts (e.g., fiction, nonfiction, myths, poems, fantasies, biographies, autobiographies, science fiction, tall tales, supernatural tales)

B. Knows the defining characteristics of a variety of literary forms and genres (e.g., fiction, nonfiction, myths, poems, fantasies, biographies, autobiographies, science fiction, tall tales, supernatural tales)

C. Identifies specific questions of personal importance and seeks to answer them through literature

D. Recognizes complex elements of plot (e.g., cause-and-effect relationships, conflicts, resolutions)

E. Recognizes devices used to develop characters in literary texts (e.g., character traits, motivations, changes, and stereotypes)

F. Makes inferences and draws conclusions about story elements (e.g., main and subordinate characters, events, setting, theme, missing details)

G. Understands complex, extended dialogues and how they relate to a story

H. Recognizes the use of specific literary devices (e.g., foreshadowing, flashback, progressive and digressive time, suspense, figurative language, description, metaphor)

I. Understands the effects of the author's style on a literary text (e.g., how it elicits an emotional response from the reader)

J. Identifies point of view in a literary text (e.g., distinguishes between first and third person)

Standards for Language Arts
Writing and Reading (cont.)

    K. Explains how the motives of characters or the causes for complex events in texts are similar to and different from those in his or her own life

    L. Understands that people respond differently to literature

7. Demonstrates competence in the general skills and strategies for reading a variety of informational texts

    A. Applies reading skills and strategies to a variety of informational texts (e.g., textbooks, biographical sketches, letters, diaries, directions, procedures, magazines, essays, primary source historical documents, editorials, news stories, periodicals, bus routes, catalogs)

    B. Summarizes and paraphrases complex, explicit hierarchic structures in informational texts

    C. Identifies information-organizing strategies that are personally most useful

    D. Uses new information to adjust and extend personal knowledge base

    E. Identifies techniques used to convey viewpoint (e.g., word choice, language structure, context)

    F. Draws conclusions and makes inferences based on explicit and implicit information in texts

Standards for Language Arts Activity Chart

	Postcards	Exit Passes	Trading Cards	Chapter/Grammar Bookmarks	Greeting Cards	Character Analysis	Important Thing	Story Scaffold	Textbook Frame	Concept Books	Flap Books	Verb Comic Strips	Bookmarks	Vocabulary Posters	Vocabulary Squares	T-Notes	Book Jackets
Writing Standards																	
1A						X	X	X	X		X		X			X	
1B	X		X	X	X	X	X										X
1C	X	X		X	X	X	X	X					X			X	X
2A					X					X							
2B	X	X	X		X		X	X	X				X				X
3A				X						X				X	X		
3B				X						X				X	X		
3C				X						X				X	X		
3D				X						X				X	X		
3E				X						X				X	X		
3F										X	X						
3G										X	X						
3A						X	X	X	X		X				X	X	
Reading Standards																	
5A	X		X					X	X		X					X	
5B	X		X			X	X	X	X		X		X			X	
5C	X		X		X					X		X	X	X	X	X	X
5D	X	X	X	X						X	X	X		X	X	X	
5E				X	X								X				X
5F	X	X	X	X	X	X	X	X	X		X		X	X	X	X	
6A	X		X		X		X	X					X				X
6B	X		X		X		X	X					X				X
6C	X	X		X	X								X			X	
6D	X		X	X	X	X	X					X		X	X	X	
6E		X		X	X	X	X						X	X		X	X
6F	X	X	X	X	X	X			X				X			X	X
6G				X		X							X			X	
6H	X						X						X	X	X		
6I	X				X		X						X				X
6J	X		X	X	X	X							X				X
6K					X	X							X			X	X
6L	X	X	X	X	X	X	X						X	X		X	X
7A		X				X	X		X		X					X	
7B	X	X	X		X		X		X		X					X	
7C							X	X					X		X	X	X
7D	X	X	X		X		X								X	X	
7E							X		X	X				X	X		
7F	X	X	X		X		X		X		X			X	X	X	

Writing a Paragraph

A well-written summary paragraph is the cornerstone for many of the activities used in this book. As space for writing is limited, it is imperative that students develop the ability to write a succinct, well-crafted paragraph.

What do students need to make a good, basic paragraph?

Topic Sentence(s): This sentence introduces the topic and/or purpose of the paragraph. Along with the introduction of the topic, the writer needs to include the purpose, main idea or reason. If students are answering a question (essay question or question from a textbook), then using part of the question in the topic sentence helps identify the topic.

Detail/Supporting Sentences: These sentences need to support or add detail, specific facts, examples, or other elaborations to the topic and its purpose. These sentences add depth to any paragraph. The number of sentences depends on the assignment, purpose, or grade level.

Concluding Sentence(s): Students need to restate the topic, make a conclusion based on the supporting facts, or, if writing additional paragraphs, transition into the next paragraph.

On page 44 is a generic paragraph scaffold handout to use with students. This scaffold contains the basic components of a paragraph, topic sentence, supporting detail sentences, and concluding statement. This is an easy outline to use when introducing paragraph writing or responding to essay questions, and can be adapted to fit any of the following five different paragraph styles.

1. **Enumeration: listing facts**

   Example: There are several layers that make up the earth. The first layer, or crust, is the earth's surface. The second layer is the mantle, which has the most mass. The outer core follows the mantle. The final layer is the molten inner core. All the different layers of the earth serve a purpose.

2. **Time order: listing events or facts in a time sequence**

   Example: John F. Kennedy's presidential legacy was marked by a number of key events. After he was elected in 1960, one of his first actions was to institute the Peace Corps. His most challenging moment was the Cuban Missile Crisis in October of 1961. Although he was assassinated in his first term of office, President Kennedy is remembered as one of the most influential leaders of our time.

Writing a Paragraph (cont.)

3. Compare-Contrast: defining same/different characteristics

Example: Writers use punctuation to stop a sentence, question, or exclamation. While a period ends a fact, a question mark leaves the reader wondering what the answer will be. Similarly, although you can use a period to end a command, an exclamation point makes that command imperative. Punctuation marks may have a similar purpose, but each supplies a different tone.

4. Cause/Effect: demonstrating how one event affects another

Example: Computers have had a major effect on the success and failure of businesses around the world. Thousands of companies rely on computers to take and prioritize orders, ship and restock products, as well as predict the trends of their clients' demands for the future. As a result, many customers look for companies to meet their individual needs with the most up-to-date technology.

5. Problem-Solution: development of a problem and its solution

Example: In *The Great Gilly Hopkins* by Katherine Paterson, Gilly's major problem is that she has moved from foster home to foster home waiting for her mother to rescue her. When this didn't happen, her solution was to antagonize and ridicule any one who tried to help soothe or comfort her. As a result, when she finally did meet her mother, Gilly realized that she had lost a family that had accepted and loved her in exchange for a mother who would never embrace her as a daughter.

Paragraph Scoring Rubric

In addition to using a scaffold as an aid, a rubric is another effective teaching tool for assessing a paragraph. An example of a four-point scoring rubric for paragraphs is on the next page.

Use the rubric as a:

1. Pre-teaching Tool: Select example paragraphs (or write your own) and use the rubric with the class to go over their strengths and weaknesses, line item by line item. It is important to have a variety of examples, including basic and below-basic components. Once you have rated a number of paragraphs with the whole class, have students work in small groups or with partners to rate paragraphs from textbooks, magazines, newspapers or non-fiction books.

2. Paragraph Writing Tool: After students have written a first draft of a paragraph using the generic paragraph scaffold or the hamburger scaffold described on the next page, assess and identify the strengths and weaknesses on the scoring rubric. This provides students with specific feedback on what needs to be revised. This would be a good time to provide mini-lessons on strong word choice, sentence structure, and conventions.

3. Published/Final Paragraphs: Incorporate the use of the rubric on all final written work. The scoring can be multiplied or weighed as part of the final assessment grade. For example, if the paragraph is worth 20 points, multiply the rubric score times five. Again, the focus should be on students' becoming familiar with using a rubric, its terminology, and how it relates to the strengths and weaknesses of their writing.

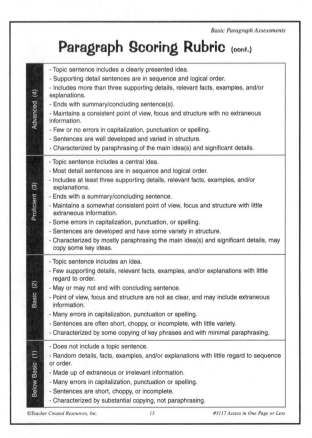

Paragraph Scoring Rubric (cont.)

Advanced (4)	- Topic sentence includes a clearly presented idea. - Supporting detail sentences are in sequence and logical order. - Includes more than three supporting details, relevant facts, examples, and/or explanations. - Ends with summary/concluding sentence(s). - Maintains a consistent point of view, focus and structure with no extraneous information. - Few or no errors in capitalization, punctuation or spelling. - Sentences are well developed and varied in structure. - Characterized by paraphrasing of the main idea(s) and significant details.
Proficient (3)	- Topic sentence includes a central idea. - Most detail sentences are in sequence and logical order. - Includes at least three supporting details, relevant facts, examples, and/or explanations. - Ends with a summary/concluding sentence. - Maintains a somewhat consistent point of view, focus and structure with little extraneous information. - Some errors in capitalization, punctuation, or spelling. - Sentences are developed and have some variety in structure. - Characterized by mostly paraphrasing the main idea(s) and significant details, may copy some key ideas.
Basic (2)	- Topic sentence includes an idea. - Few supporting details, relevant facts, examples, and/or explanations with little regard to order. - May or may not end with concluding sentence. - Point of view, focus and structure are not as clear, and may include extraneous information. - Many errors in capitalization, punctuation or spelling. - Sentences are often short, choppy, or incomplete, with little variety. - Characterized by some copying of key phrases and with minimal paraphrasing.
Below Basic (1)	- Does not include a topic sentence. - Random details, facts, examples, and/or explanations with little regard to sequence or order. - Made up of extraneous or irrelevant information. - Many errors in capitalization, punctuation or spelling. - Sentences are short, choppy, or incomplete. - Characterized by substantial copying, not paraphrasing.

Paragraph Scaffold – Hamburger Style

The following "hamburger" scaffolding framework is not new but can be particularly useful to assist middle school students in paragraph writing. The scaffold can be used as a pre-writing exercise or an introduction to paragraph writing. Have students practice using the format at the beginning of the year whenever they answer essay or analytical questions, or when writing short expository or informational paragraphs. Later in the year, the format can be expanded and adapted for an entire essay. See the Bite into Writing Student Instructions on page 45.

The **bun** is equated with the topic sentence. If students are responding to a question, they should restate the question in their answer so as to guide the reader.

The **lettuce** should be the reason for their answer. This should be stated in one to two sentences. It can be a personal opinion, or a fact.

The **beef** is the "meat" of the paragraph. This should consist of an explanation, an example, along with elaboration and perhaps analysis.

The **bun** on the bottom finishes the paragraph by restating the answer, summarizing, or, for the more advanced writer, transitioning to the next paragraph.

For more advanced students, more elements can be added to fill out the paragraph. For example, when students begin to analyze literature, they can add analysis as an onion slice to their burger. The hamburger format can also be expanded to cover an entire essay. For multiple paragraph essays, the lettuce, beef, and onion slices are repeated. Teaching this format saves a lot of work in the long run. When correcting student paragraphs or essays, students can be told that they are missing the lettuce (topic sentence) or onion (analysis), or that they need to "beef" up their essays with more facts and examples.

Blank Postcards

What can you do with only one-fourth of a page? Lots of things! Here are some favorite ideas, but you can change and adapt them to fit the needs of your students.

Use the template on page 46 to complete these activities. On the blank side, have students create a visual, colorful representation of a concept. On the other side, students write a summary paragraph or explanation, list facts, or outline a topic. See pages 10–14 for suggestions on how to write a general summary paragraph. English Language Learner teachers have found the postcards with the picture a useful alternative method to assess concept development with minimal writing. Once the postcards have been assessed, mail them to the parents to easily improve the school-to-home connection. Here are a few ideas to get you started:

Curriculum Connections

Science: Students draw a picture of a concept (such as erosion), scientific method, or an element, on the blank side of the postcard. On the other side, they address the postcard to their parents, and write a short explanation about the concept.

Social Studies: Students draw a picture of an historical figure or event on the blank side of the postcard. They address the card to another famous person in that time period, and write a short narrative explaining their view of the historical event or the significance of the famous person.

Language Arts: After reading a novel or short story, students draw a setting, character, or problem. On the back of the postcard, students write an explanation or description of the picture to the story line. Or, have them assume the point of view of a character and retell their role in the plot and address the card to another character (or the author).

The samples on the next page provide additional ideas.

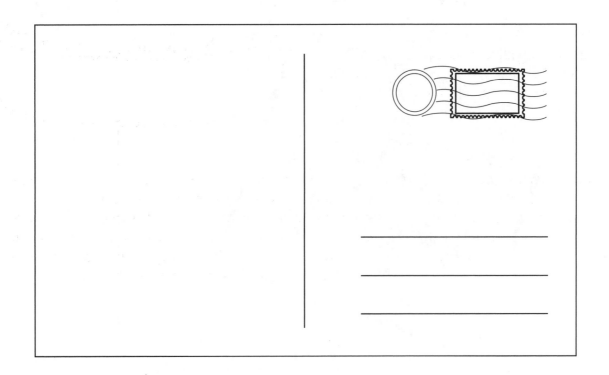

Blank Postcards (cont.)

Sample Postcards

Today I Learned Postcards

You can find this template on page 47. Much like the blank postcard on page 46, this format directs students to identify, picture, and summarize an essential idea or concept, starting their paragraph with the "Today I Learned…" stem. Once the students have shared their postcards with you or their classmates, or posted them in the classroom, forward them to an interested parent or principal.

Curriculum Connections

Science: Students draw and label the earth's different layers on the front of the postcard. On the back, they summarize each layer with specific details about composition and depth.

Social Studies: As an introduction, assign each student a different picture from the textbook chapters for a specific unit or culture. Each student recreates the picture on the front, and describes the importance of the picture on the back. Students can then share their cards in class for an overview before reading or starting a unit.

Language Arts: To assess a reading or homework assignment, select an element of the story, such as character development, conflict, setting, or climax. After reading, students draw a picture that represents that story element, and write a summary paragraph of what they read on the back.

Sample Today I Learned Postcards

Exit Passes

Exit passes can be the students' "ticket out the door" and provide a quick demonstration of what they learned that period. Spend the last five minutes of class having students summarize, list, explain, or describe what was presented during the period, using the Exit Pass template on page 48. You can quickly categorize responses to determine which students are in need of additional help, as well as hold the students accountable for listening and daily classroom work.

Or, personalize the exit pass for a specific reading assignment, concept or idea. Prior to class, prepare specific true/false or open-ended questions to guide responses.

Curriculum Connections

Science: Create an exit pass with 5–7 true/false questions about the reading, concept, or lesson for the day. At the end of class, each student completes a pass (like a mini-quiz). This will give you immediate feedback on what students understood, and what, if any, concept needs to be revisited.

Social Studies: After a movie or lecture, have students record on the exit pass the most important concept(s) or idea(s) in paragraph format. Before class begins, you can also have students write focus questions on a specific topic that will be highlighted during that period.

Language Arts: Highlight important vocabulary words or terms for the day (such as literary devices, parts of speech, spelling rules). At the end of the period, have students write the definitions or use the words or terms in sentences to demonstrate understanding.

Exit Pass

What you must know to leave class today!

1.
   _____
   _____
   _____

2.
   _____
   _____
   _____

3.
   _____
   _____
   _____

Exit Passes (cont.)

Sample Exit Passes

Exit Pass

What you must know to leave class today!

1.   **What is gravity?**

_____

_____

2..   **What is mass?**

_____

_____

3..   **What is friction?**

_____

_____

Exit Pass

What you must know to leave class today!

Answer the following questions:

Who is the narrator of "The Tell-Tale Heart"?

The main character—not named

From what point of view is the story told?

first person

What literary elements increase the tension in the story?

repetition, short, choppy sentences, irony

Exit Pass

What you must know to leave class today!

Write the definitions for the following literary terms:

Plot

sequence of events that make up the story

Setting

time and place where the action happened

Point of view

vantage point from which a story is told

Climax

point in the story that reveals how the conflict turns out.

Exit Pass

What you must know to leave class today!

Answer the following questions:

T   F

☐ ☐   Friction is caused by hills and valleys on surfaces.

☐ ☐   Without friction, things would move more easily.

☐ ☐   Gravity is a result of mass.

☐ ☐   If an elephant and a mouse jump off a building, they would hit the ground at the same time.

Trading Cards

Just like sport trading cards from the past, students can create cards describing key concepts, characters or people using the templates on pages 49–52. On the framed side (front), have students design a player, such as a character from a book or famous historical person. On the back, students can write a description. Key events, concepts or ideas can also be illustrated on the front, with definitions and examples on the reverse side. These cards can then be shared by students when reviewing the unit or studying for a test.

Curriculum Connections

Science: Assign each student an element from the periodic table. Each student can then make a trading card with an illustration of molecules of the element on the front and specific facts on the back.

Social Studies: For a unit such as Greece, have each student make a card for a key cultural component. Examples for the front of the card could be a map of Greece for geography, a picture of Zeus for religion, a symbol of democracy representing government, and so forth. On the back of the card, have the student explain the symbolic picture and its importance in the civilization.

Language Arts: Characters come alive when students create trading cards about them while reading a book or short story. Include a picture on one side with a description of the character and his or her importance on the reverse. In addition, make flash cards for key vocabulary words, spelling words, literary devices (metaphors, similes, alliteration, etc.), or parts of speech. Sample sentences or examples could be on one side, and definitions on the other.

As a writing extension, have students create trading cards for a main character, setting, problem or conflict, and resolution. All the cards can be mixed up, then students can pick different character, setting, conflict and resolution cards, and write short stories to fit the elements.

Trading Cards (cont.)

Sample Trading Cards

Edgar Allan Poe

Edgar Allan Poe
- Born in Boston 1809 - 1849,
- orphan before he was 3
- adopted by the Allan family and received a good education
- published two volumes of poetry by age 20
- famous for tales of horror and mystery
- famous works include "The Raven", "The Pit and the Pendulum", The Fall of the House of Usher" and "The Tell-Tale Heart"

Metaphor

An imaginative comparison between two unlikely things in which one thing is said to be another thing.

- He was a mountain of a man.

- She was an angel

- The night was a dark cloak

Her eyes were blue stars.

Metaphor

Chapter and Grammar Bookmarks

Divide a piece of paper into thirds and you have bookmarks that can be used for multiple purposes.

Use the blank template on page 53 for chapters in a novel or literature book, Customize the template with specific questions, general reading and comprehension responses, or chapter summaries. Write your questions in by hand, or set up the basic format in your computer. Students can keep the markers in their books for easy review when they are done reading.

Language Arts Connections

For any novel, develop a bookmark for each chapter with a question for students to reflect on before they read the chapter, a question to answer during their reading, and a question for reflection after. A "before" question could include making a prediction on what will happen to the character in the chapter. A "during" activity could include identifying key vocabulary words, as well as their definitions and importance in the story line. An "after" reflection could ask students to retell the three most important events from the chapter, and why each event was important.

Another idea is to identify parts of speech and their use in a reading selection. For example, have students identify a key noun (person, place, or thing) for the story. On the bookmark, have students explain why that noun is important. Additional bookmarks could explain other parts of speech, including a verb (action of story), adjective (describing character or setting), adverb (how character acts), preposition (where key event or climax happened), etc. (See the samples on page 23.)

Your readers can also design their own bookmarks, by drawing the setting or key characters, writing story summaries, or retelling the plot development. Incorporate your literature book anthologies by having a bookmark for different types of stories (biography, non-fiction, poetry, historical fiction, etc.) with specific genre-related questions. Assign the students to select different types of stories in an anthology, and have them do a bookmark for each one.

Sample Bookmarks

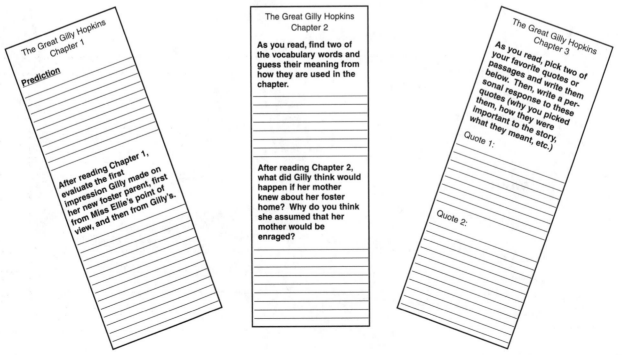

Chapter and Grammar Bookmarks (cont.)

Sample Bookmarks

Hood, n.

In "Little Red Riding Hood", the main character is Little Red Riding Hood. She is defined by the distinctive red hood that she wears. This hood is important because the wolf not only recognizes her as she walks through the woods wearing the hood, but it is his disguise. He tricks the Grandmother to let him in when he dresses as Little Red Riding Hood.

In the end, however, the original red-hood wearer is successful in saving herself and her grandmother to live happily ever after in her hood.

Crafty, adj.

"Little Red Riding Hood" is a story about some very crafty characters.

To begin with, the wolf is one smart, crafty fellow who tried to outsmart both Little Red Riding Hood, as well as her grandmother.

He almost succeeds in getting the basket, the grandmother, and Red by his crafty moves. However, Little Red Riding Hood figures out his plan, and by her own crafty ability, is able to save herself and her grandmother.

Eat, v.

"Little Red Riding Hood" is about a poor, defenseless young girl, Little Red, who is bringing her grandmother something to eat, and must escape being eaten by the Big Bad Wolf.

Unfortunately, she meets up with the wolf on her way to her grandmother's house. Seeing his opportunity, the wolf beats Red to her grandmother's house and locks the grandmother in a closet.

Before the wolf can eat her, Red enlists the aid of a passing woodcutter, who saves the day by killing the wolf and freeing the grandmother. The story ends with them all eating the basket of goodies.

Postcards, Exit Passes, and Greeting Cards

Assessment possibilities are endless when you have a half a piece of paper.

• Postcards

These are just like the quarter-page postcards described earlier, however, the templates on pages 54 and 55 are bigger, allowing for more in-depth writing, including summaries, letters to characters, or students recording what they learned.

• Exit Passes

Previously explained in the quarter page section, the half page exit templates on pages 56, 57, and 58 provide more room for additional questions or detailed writing for an exit reflection.

• Greeting Cards

Identifying the different points of view from a story allows students to delve more deeply into a character's actions and reveals a better understanding of the plot and theme. Or, in a content area, a different point of view is a creative opportunity for the class to assume the role of an historical figure, inventor or scientist. Have students create a variety of greeting cards, such as thank-you notes, or sympathy, congratulations, birthday greetings, wish-you-were-here, happy anniversary, or friendship cards to help reveal their understanding of important events or changes, and the people affected. No template is required—all you need is a half piece of paper that is folded to make a card (try using colored construction paper for more variety). Many computer programs also have card-making capabilities that can be utilized for this activity.

Curriculum Connections

Science: Each student is assigned a different inventor. Students must make 2-3 cards that have symbolic, colorful fronts, with messages revealing important facts or consequences of their inventor's inventions. For example, Edison could write a "wish-you-were-here" card to his parents explaining how he would like to see them using his new light bulb. Or, Edison could send a friendship card to his lab partner, Watson, asking him to come see him.

Postcards, Exit Passes, and Greeting Cards (cont.)

• Greeting Cards (cont.)

Social Studies: Pass out names of important historical leaders or famous people from a time period or unit, and have students send greeting cards from one historical figure to another. Anthony could send Cleopatra a love note, Brutus could forward a sympathy card to Caesar, or George Washington could write a telegram to his troops, and so forth.

Language Arts: Fables and myths usually provide rich and descriptive characters who could send interesting greeting cards. Or, from the point of view of a main character in a novel, students could create at least five different cards to send to minor characters in the story revealing an event, action, or emotional shift, and why it was important. Or, for a twist, have the class assume the role of an inanimate object, like a period, comma, question mark or exclamation point, and have them write to another type of punctuation.

Greeting Card Sample

Dear Persephone,

Because you ate those pomegranate seeds,
In one more month,
My call you must heed.
I love you so much,
My "Princess of Spring,"
I'm quite certain that you will make a great Queen.

Your Loving King

Hades

Character Analysis Boxes

Use the template on page 59 to help students uncover a deeper understanding of a character. The Character Analysis Boxes work best for literature books or stories and help students better analyze a character, not just how they look or act, but how a person's thoughts and feelings reflect and influence the story line. As a pre-writing activity for a student-created narrative story or fable, students can use the character analysis template to sketch out their main characters.

Character Analysis Box Sample

Character Analysis

Use the boxes below to record information about your character

Appearance	Actions
cracked, dirty shoes legs wrapped in rags black, heavily wrinkled face crinkly white hair	picking through trash stood up to bullies
Thoughts/Feelings	**Dialogue**
"You know your pappy did something, so you know you can do something, too." Son was killed, broke his heart	"I got me a razor" "Every man got a treasure"
Others' reactions	**Author's Direct Statements**
"Throw down your money so we won't have to hurt you."	old man

"The Important Thing" Scaffold

Picture books are always quick resources for teachers to read to assist students in grasping a concept or idea. One book, *The Important Book* by Margaret Wise Brown, has a basic format that can be turned into a powerful scaffold for any age. The template on page 60 outlines the fill-in-the blank response to use. First, read *The Important Book* so students can understand the pattern and principle. Then, have students use the scaffold handout for any fiction or non-fiction reading. The purpose is for students to identify the main idea/purpose of their reading, as well as describe minor details or supporting facts.

Curriculum Connections

Science: Use with any article or chapter reading.

Social Studies: Have students use "The Important Thing" scaffold for important events, people, or cultural components.

Language Arts: Highlight a character or differentiate between the climax and other events in a story using the scaffold. Have students create one for the character, setting, conflict, or other story elements.

"The Important Thing" Scaffold Sample

Name _____ Date _____

"The Important Thing"

Topic

_____

The important thing about

   The geography of Egypt

is that

   The Nile River was the lifeline of the Egyptian culture.

_____

_____

It is true that

   The Nile River provided water for farming and drinking,

   a method of transportation, and fish for eating.

But the important thing about

   The Nile River

is that

   It provided a lifeline to the Egyptians.

_____

_____

Story Scaffold Framework

Use the story frame and scaffold template on page 61 to retell a story, describe a character, summarize a plot, or relate conflicts or problems and how they were solved—in other words, have students reflect and respond to aspects of a story while they are reading it or after they have finished it.

Story Scaffold Framework Sample

Name _____ Date _____

Story Scaffold

Title of Story <u>Little Red Riding Hood</u>

The Story begins when...

<u>Red Riding Hood sets off through the forest to</u>
<u>bring her grandmother a basket of food.</u>

The problem is…

<u>There's a wolf in the woods that is dangerous.</u>

The next thing that happened is…

<u>The wolf distracts Red and she delays her visit to</u>
<u>grandmother's.</u>

Then…

<u>The wolf gets to grandmother's first, puts her in</u>
<u>the closet and lays waiting for Red disguised as</u>
<u>grandmother.</u>

After that…

<u>Red arrives. The wolf, disguised, tries to eat Little</u>
<u>Red Riding Hood.</u>

the problem is solved when

<u>A hunter hears the noise and kills the wolf.</u>

Textbook Frame

The reading framework template on page 62 is designed for a content-related textbook chapter, such as social studies or science. When finished, this reading scaffolding pattern can be used as support to write a summary paragraph of what was read.

Textbook Frame Sample

Name:_____ Date:_____

Question

During the Neolithic Era, or New Stone Age, why were people able to settle permanently in one location?

Response:

1. Topic Sentence

People in the New Stone Age were able to build cities because they learned how to manage agriculture and workers started to specialize.

2. Supporting Detail Sentence

A major breakthrough was when they learned to domesticate plants and animals. As a result, farmers had a planned food supply as well as surplus for winter.

3. Supporting Detail Sentence

The surplus of food allowed other people to specialize in other types of work besides farming. Other jobs included craft workers and traders.

4. Supporting Detail Sentence

The changes in the community jobs also sparked a change and growth into a more advanced civilization that included religion and government.

5. Summary/Conclusion Sentence

In conclusion, the ability of people during the Neolithic Era to control their food supply changed the primitive cultures into more permanent advanced civilizations.

Concept Books

Everyone enjoys seeing his or her work displayed or published. You can quickly bind almost any half- (or full-) sheet activity to keep as a classroom display. Concepts that always need new ideas to keep students interested are grammar and literary devices, or other language mechanics.

• Grammar Books

Students can demonstrate their grammar skills through sentence writing and diagramming on half sheets of paper. As shown in the examples below and on the next page, students can write sentences and then underline, label, and diagram the part of speech being emphasized. See the student direction sheets found on pages 63-67 for a variety of grammar and language convention possibilities, including nouns, verbs, adjectives, prepositions, and adverbs. For future review and enjoyment, teachers can collect all the student samples and bind them into a classroom book.

Sample Grammar Books

Concept Books (cont.)

Sample Grammar Books (cont.)

The wolves sat <u>anxiously</u> in the snow, as the two hares ran <u>very</u> fast, but the wolves were <u>faster</u>.

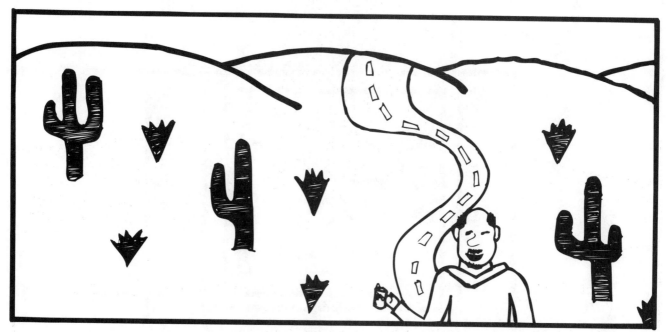

The awkward man <u>slowly</u> walked down the <u>very</u> windy street drinking a <u>not so</u> big can of soda <u>ever so</u> <u>quickly</u>.

Concept Books (cont.)

• Literary Devices and Language Mechanics

In addition to reinforcing grammar skills, use the Concept Book format for literary or writing techniques, such as alliteration, clichés, or idioms. See the student instructions for idioms on page 68.

Expand into other language mechanics activities, like identifying types of sentences, by providing students with animal pictures from "National Geographic," "Ranger Rick," or any other magazine and then have them identify and write different kinds of sentences (declarative, interrogative, imperative, and exclamatory) to match the situation. See the student directions for the activity on page 69 and samples on the next page.

Curriculum Connections

Science: Divide among the students key terms or vocabulary words for a unit. Have students work individually or in pairs to create books on these important concepts.

Social Studies: Book ideas could include famous people from an era, important dates and events, or geographical terms.

Language Arts: Create an "About the Author" class book of all your students. On the front side, students can use examples found on the inside of most book jackets as a guide to writing short biographies about themselves in the third person. On the reverse side of the page, students can draw pictures of themselves, bring in photographs, or (if you have a digital camera in your classroom) take photos and place them on each biography. This "About the Author" book can be expanded to a one-page format. Students can write or type their biography on a half-sheet of paper, glue it to the bottom half of a colored sheet of paper, and add the picture to the top.

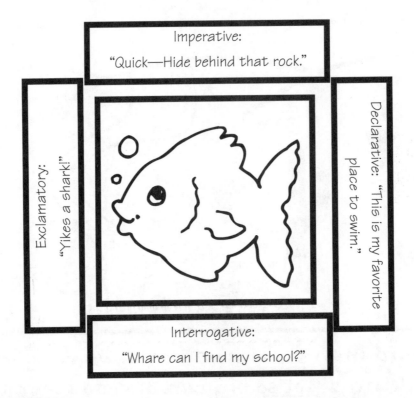

Concept Books (cont.)

Sample Literary Devices and Language Mechanics Books (cont.)

Flap Books

Take two, three or four ½ sheets of paper, layer them about ½ inch apart, fold over, staple, and you have easy-to-use "flap" books to record notes, main ideas with supporting facts under the flap, or label with punctuation or capitalization rules and sentence examples. Flap books can help students break down a big topic into smaller, easier chunks. The instruction sheet on page 70 is for capitalization rules, but you can adapt the book for almost any information.

Curriculum Connections

Science: Use books to collect notes for an informational report by placing the thesis statement on the top flap, and three supporting details on the following flap headings. On each detail flap, students can list specific examples, facts, and researched information for each supporting detail. Paragraphs can then be easily written from the organized notes.

Social Studies: For a textbook chapter, place the chapter title on the front and then have students write section headings or main ideas for each flap heading and record details and facts under the flaps as they read.

Language Arts: Much like the "cap flap" example, use the flap book for comma rules, listing the 5-7 key comma rules on the flap headings, with sample example sentences underneath the flap demonstrating the rule.

Sample Flap Books

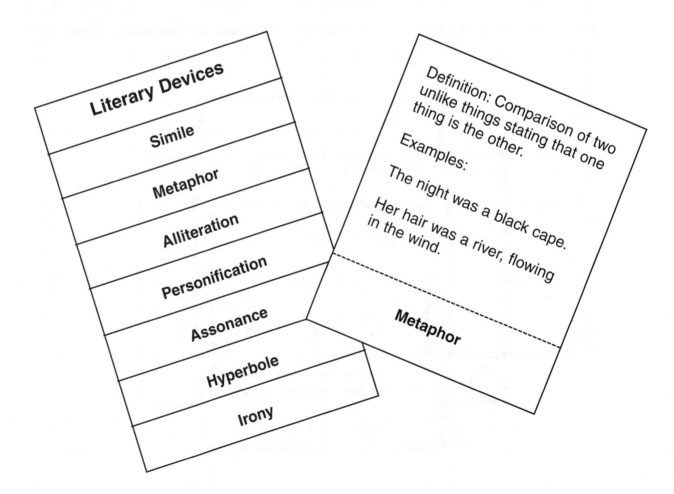

Flap Books (cont.)

Sample Flap Books (cont.)

Comma Flap

Rule #1 Use commas to separate items in a series. Items in a series may be words, phrases, or clauses.

Rule #2 Use commas to separate two or more adjectives that come before a noun. (Test: insert "and" between adjectives. If it sounds awkward, don't use a comma.)

Rule #3 Use a comma before and, but, for, so, yet, and or when they join independent clauses in a compound sentence.

Rule #4 Use commas to set off an appositive. An appositive follows the noun and renames it. Appositives are used to give more information.

Rule #5 Use commas to set off the names used in a direct address. (Direct address is using the name of the person to whom you are speaking.)

Rule #6 If yes, no, or well begin a sentence, use a comma after them.

Rule #7 Use commas in certain conventional situations. For example, to separate dates and addresses, after the salutation in a friendly letter, or after the closing of a letter.

Verb Comic Strips

These forms and templates allow for more detail and information, but are still excellent and quick assessment tools.

Much like the grammar books described on page 30, students demonstrate their knowledge of the different types of verbs using their favorite animal in a comic strip. (See the student directions on page 71.) Bind all the comics into a class book.

Sample Verb Comic Strip

Full-page Bookmarks

Use the templates on page 72–75 as the larger versions of bookmarks for novels or short stories. Copy the templates back-to-back and fold them so students can keep them in their books. These large bookmarks are useful tools for students to use as they read, helping them to recognize and define plot elements, important events, and meaningful quotes. Students can turn in their bookmarks with their final book reviews or reports.

Sample Full-page Bookmarks

What is the main conflict in this story? Explain.

The main conflict in the story is how Matilda and her classmates try to live and go to school with evil Mrs. Trunchbull and get along with her, which is very hard.

What kind of conflict is it? Explain. (Internal, External? Man vs. Man, Man vs. Society, Man vs. Self, Man vs. Nature?)

I think it's man vs. man because it's the kids against the adults in the book.

**Plot Summary:
Rising Action/Complications:**

The rising action is when Matilda notices that she has some kind of special power that by staring at something she is able to make it move or lift.

Climax

The climax is when Matilda makes chalk write on the board using her powers and the writing is a secret about the headmistress' evil life.

Falling Action/Resolution

The headmistress falls and faints, and after that incident left her house which was supposed to be Miss Honey's.

What is the Theme, or Main Idea of this story?

I think the main idea of the story is that there are good people like Miss Honey, who is kind and helpful, and evil people like Mrs. Trunchbull, who is more of a monster.

Roald Dahl
Author's Name

The Book I'm Reading is Titled:
Matilda

This Author Has also Written:
James and the Giant Peach

Exposition: Describe the setting:

This story takes place in different parts of the city Matilda lives in like the library, school, and home.

What inferences can you make from the title, the characters' names, the format, the setting, or the first paragraph? (Can you guess what the story will be about from these?)

The first paragraph talks about a girl genius who has idiotic parents.

Exposition: The Main Characters Are (Give a short description of each)

Matilda: the main character, very intelligent. Mr. and Mrs. Wormwood: Matilda's parents, unfair and ignorant. Miss Honey: Matilda's teacher, kind, loving, quiet, and respectful. Mrs. Trunchbull: headmistress of Matilda's school, evil, mean, old, and hates children. Nigel and Lavender: classmates from Matilda's grade who are always in trouble.

Vocabulary Poster

Spice up your vocabulary words and your classroom with creative posters of important terms. Students are assigned key vocabulary words and, using a white piece of paper, make a colorful, symbolic poster. For each word, students need to draw a border that creatively uses the word. On the top and bottom of the paper, students write the definition and part of speech, then use the word in a sentence. In the middle of the paper, in large letters, students symbolically write the word using bubble, creative, or logo-type lettering that also shows the meaning of the word. For example, if the term was "disappear," letters of the word could gradually disappear off the page. Encourage abstract, creative thinking to interpret word meaning through creative word art. See the student directions on page 76.

Sample Vocabulary Posters

Vocabulary Square

This versatile vocabulary square template on page 77 allows you to change the information required for each word. Select terms that are key to understanding a unit or concept. Science or social studies teachers can identify content-related terms, or key language arts concepts or vocabulary. Each word needs to have four supporting details assigned by the teacher. Details for each word could include: definition, picture of word, importance of word to story or concept, synonyms, antonyms, examples, part of speech, or use in a sentence.

Curriculum Connections

Science: In the study of rocks, have students place the three different categories of rocks: igneous, metamorphic, and sedimentary, in three of the middle boxes. For a fourth word, select another key term, such as erosion. For the descriptors, have students 1) write the definition, 2) list examples, 3) draw a picture illustrating the word, and 4) describe its uses.

Social Studies: During a unit study, such as Egypt, pick four terms (e.g., Shadouf, Upper Egypt, Lower Egypt, Nile River) and place them in the middle boxes. Details for descriptor boxes could be definition, picture, importance to ancient Egypt, and use in a sentence.

Language Arts: When studying poetry (or the use of literary devices), introduce important descriptive writing techniques using the vocabulary square. Example terms could include simile, metaphor, alliteration, and onomatopoeia; with supporting details of a definition, student example(s), published example(s) from a poem, and their importance in descriptive writing (what they add). Or, select a key word from a novel and, in the four descriptor boxes, have students describe how the word is important to the setting, character development, theme, and conflict.

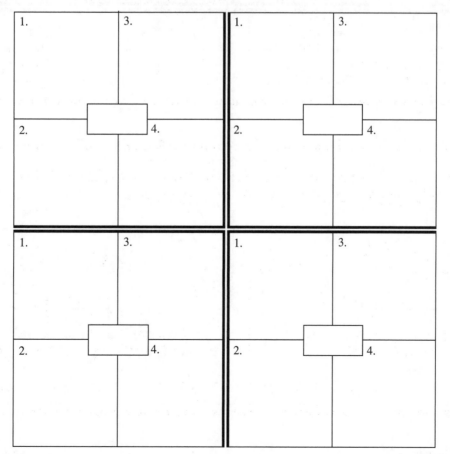

Vocabulary Square (cont.)

Vocabulary Square Sample

Vocabulary Square

1. Farmers scooped water from canals and poured it into the fields using a bucket lifter called a shadouf.

3. The shadouf was important in Egypt because the water and mud it scooped provided minerals to grow plants to feed Egypt.

Shadouf

2.

4. The shadouf scoop's water from canals to feed plants.

---

1. The Nile/Delta region is in Northern Egypt and appears nearer the top on maps. This makes the Delta seem higher. The Delta is lower Egypt where the Nile flows up to the Mediterranean Sea, that is where upper Egypt is.

3. Upper Egypt was home to people who lived there with lots of rich minerals to trade.

Upper Egypt

2.

4. Upper Egypt is a place where Merchants lived and ruled. There are many villagers there.

---

1. The Nile/Delta region is in northern Egypt and appears nearer the top on maps. This makes the Delta seem higher, however the Delta is called lower Egypt.

3. Lower Egypt was home and important to many people. The Delta had canals to feed the crops.

Lower Egypt (Delta)

2.

4. Lower Egypt was home and a place to live near the capital.

---

1. The Nile River wound through the vast desert with a few signs of life. The river was the most important water source to the Egyptians.

3. The Nile fed, washed watered, etc...in Egypt and was a key to travel.

Nile River

2.

4. The Nile River feeds the Egyptians and also helped grow plants with water.

---

1. definition

2. draw a picture

3. describe its geographical importance in Egypt

4. use in a sentence

T-Notes

The template on page 78 is a simple note-taking format that has a multitude of purposes, including use as a response journal, recording main ideas and details, question and answer sheet, and problem/solution or cause/effect identification. Teachers can also prepare the left side in advance to help guide the response column on the right.

See the list of ideas on the following page.

Curriculum Connections

Science: Students title "cause" on left-hand column, and "effect" on the right. During an experiment, have students record the steps, noting the addition (cause) and the change (effect).

Social Studies: Before duplicating the form, the teacher writes 5–7 questions in the left-hand column that will be covered from a lesson, chapter or article. During the reading, students answer the questions in the right-hand column, using complete sentences, including page numbers.

Language Arts: Use as a response journal. As students read a chapter or selection, they need to select and record three direct quotes in the left-hand column. In the right, using complete paragraph(s), have them detail why each quote was important to the story.

T-Notes Sample

Literary Term/Key Words	Definition/Example
Alliteration repeat consonant sounds	Repetition of consonant sounds in words that are close together. "Six slimy snakes slithered silently"
Allusion reference	A reference to a statement, a person, place, or event from literature, the arts, history, or culture. "She was as smart as Einstein"
Dialect way of speaking	A way of speaking that is characteristic of a certain geographical area or a certain group of people. "Y'all come back real soon" "G'day mate!"
Figure of Speech use for description/metaphor, simile, personification	A word or phrase that describes one thing in terms of another and is not meant to be understood as literally true "the sun smiled down on me"
Symbol one thing stands for another	A person, place, thing or event that has meaning in itself and stands for something beyond itself as well. dove = peace/freedom

T-Notes (cont.)

Two-column notes (T-Notes) can be adapted to any setting or situation to meet a specific purpose. Remember to include heading and t-note titles. Here are some examples (but the list could go on).

1. **What I Know/What I Want to Know**

   Introduce a new concept or chapter, or activate background knowledge.

2. **Questions/Answers**

   To prepare for tests or review chapters, students can generate questions and then answer them.

3. **Big Questions/Small Questions**

   Introduce the big questions (big ideas/focus) for unit, and then brainstorm or generate smaller, related questions that will help answer the big questions.

4. **Direct Quote/Personal Response**

   Have students select a direct quote from text (fiction or non-fiction) and then explain their personal response to the quote.

5. **What the Text Is About/What I Think About it**

   Have students write main ideas or concepts and then what they think about them, or their connection to information.

6. **Opinion/Proof**

   Students can form opinions or predictions, and then look for the proof in the text or story.

7. **Problem/Solution**

   This can include math problems and solutions or character problems and solutions.

8. **Familiar Concept/New Concept**

   As students read, they can record familiar concepts on one side, and new concepts or information on the other.

9. **Topic/Detail**

   Main ideas, section titles, subtitles, concepts or key words, and supporting details can be recorded.

Book Jacket

Use the directions and template on pages 79 and 80 for this activity. Although you can use an 8 ½" x 11" piece of paper for this response-to-literature activity, a longer, narrower piece of paper (such as 12" x 18") results in a better quality product. Use this activity for a detailed book report that highlights all the different parts of a story: character, setting, problem/solution, story summary, and genre identification. Note: this report usually takes 2–3 class periods, or can be used as a culminating independent project.

Book Jacket Sample

Paragraph Writing Student Instructions

1. Restate the question or introduce your topic in the first sentence of your answer. Let your reader know, in the very first sentence, exactly what you're going to talk about.

    Q: *Of all the types of novels, which genre is your favorite?*

    A: *Of all the types of novels, mysteries are my favorite.*

2. Give a reason for your answer.

    A: *I love mysteries because I love the feeling of fear and suspense.*

3. Explain your reason or give an example. Your reason should have at least two sentences to explain it. In longer writing, you will need more sentences.

    A: *It's amazing to be reading a book and be so wrapped up in the action that you actually get a tingle down your spine and fear goes through your body when the main character is in danger. And nothing is better than a book that is so suspenseful that you can't put it down—not even when your favorite TV show is on!*

4. Restate your answer, summarize your thoughts, or transition to next paragraph. Summarize your answer, add a final thought or statement, and lead into the next paragraph.

    A: *Although I like to read all types of novels, I enjoy the excitement that I experience when I read mysteries.*

Now you try it! Answer the question your teacher gives you using the box below. Follow the numbered guidelines!

1. _____

   _____

2. _____

   _____

3. _____

   _____

4. _____

   _____

Bite into Writing Student Instructions

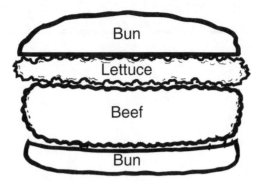

Bun—Introduction. Restate the questions in your answer, or give a little background to introduce your topic.

Lettuce—Thesis or Topic Sentence. Give a reason for your answer, or state your thesis.

Beef —Body of paragraph. This is the meat of your answer! Explain, give an example, elaborate, analyze. This part will be at least 2–3 sentences and can be as big as necessary to explain your reason.

Bun—Conclusion. Wrap it up: summarize or transition to next paragraph.

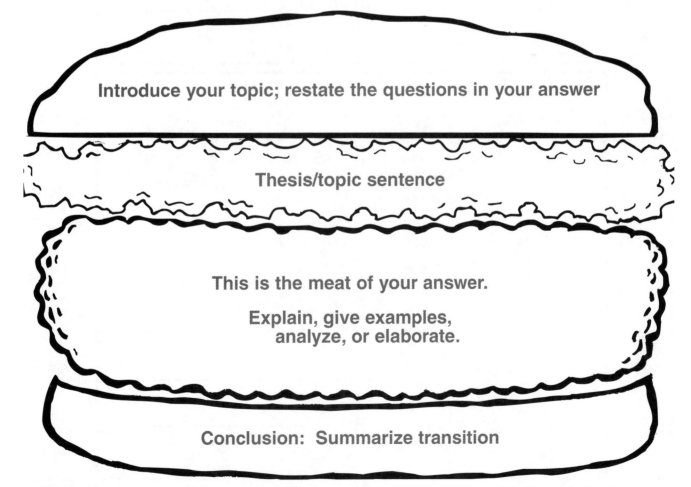

Introduce your topic; restate the questions in your answer

Thesis/topic sentence

This is the meat of your answer.

Explain, give examples,
analyze, or elaborate.

Conclusion: Summarize transition

Blank Postcard Template

Copy this page twice. Paste four templates onto one 8½" x 11" sheet of paper. Use that paper as a master.

"Today I Learned" Postcard Template

Copy this page twice. Paste four templates onto one 8½" x 11" sheet of paper. Use that paper as a master.

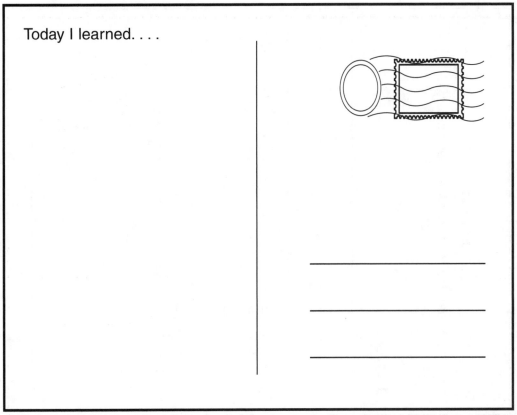

Today I learned. . . .

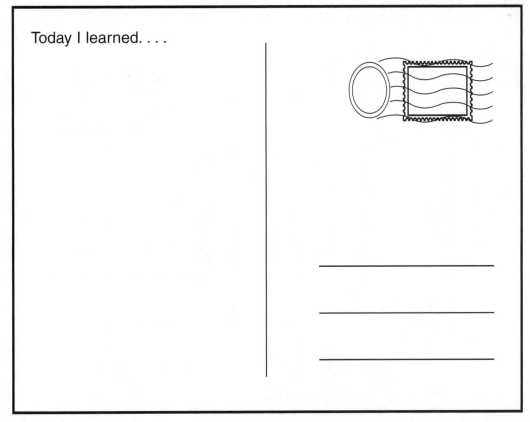

Today I learned. . . .

Exit Pass Template

Copy this page twice. Paste four templates onto one 8½" x 11" sheet of paper. Use that paper as a master.

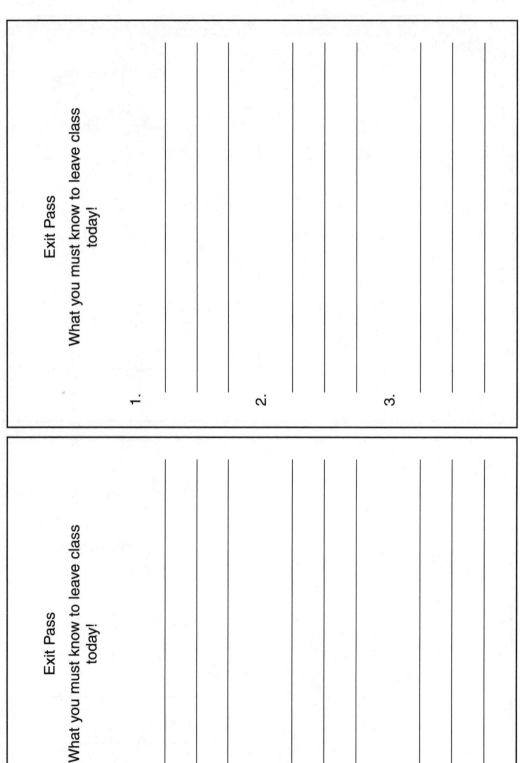

Trading Cards Templates

Create a master copy by copying the trading cards below twice and pasting four cards on one 8 ½" x 11" page. You may also mix and match the trading cards on the next three pages.

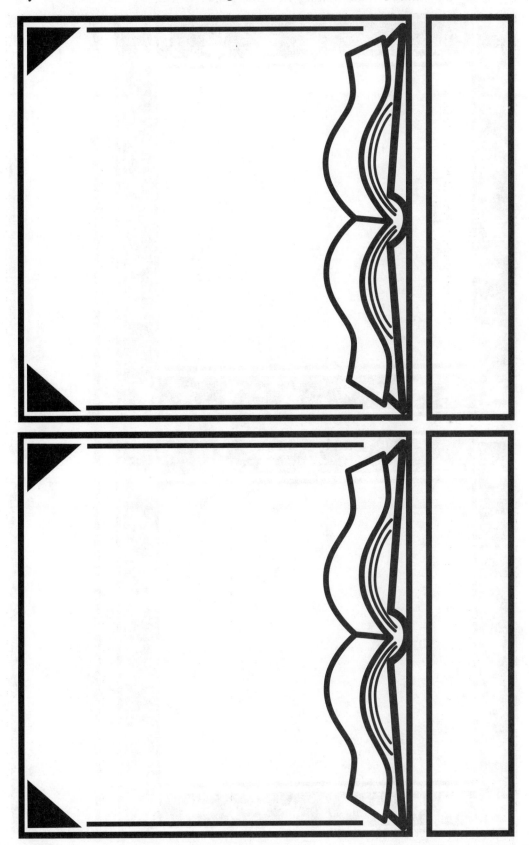

Trading Cards Templates (cont.)

Create a master copy by copying the trading cards below twice and pasting four cards on one 8 ½" x 11" page. You may also mix and match the trading cards on pages 49–52.

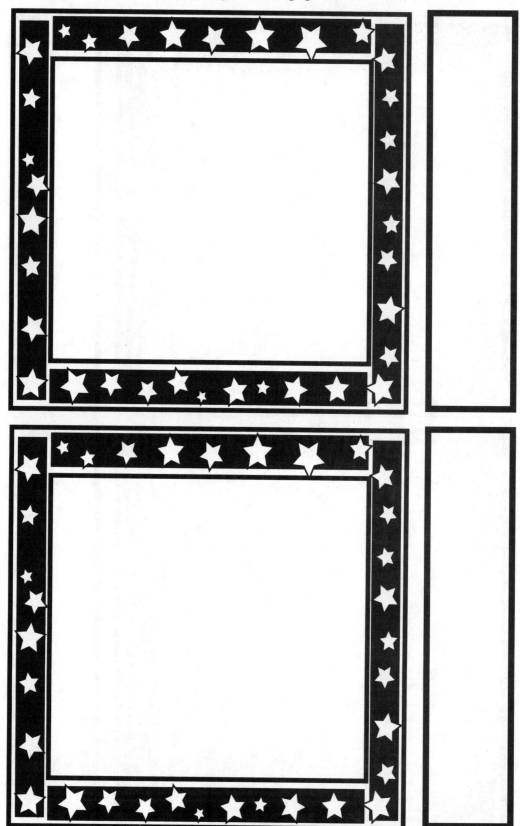

Trading Cards Template (cont.)

Create a master copy by copying the trading cards below twice and pasting four cards on one 8 ½" x 11" page. You may also mix and match the trading cards on pages 49–52.

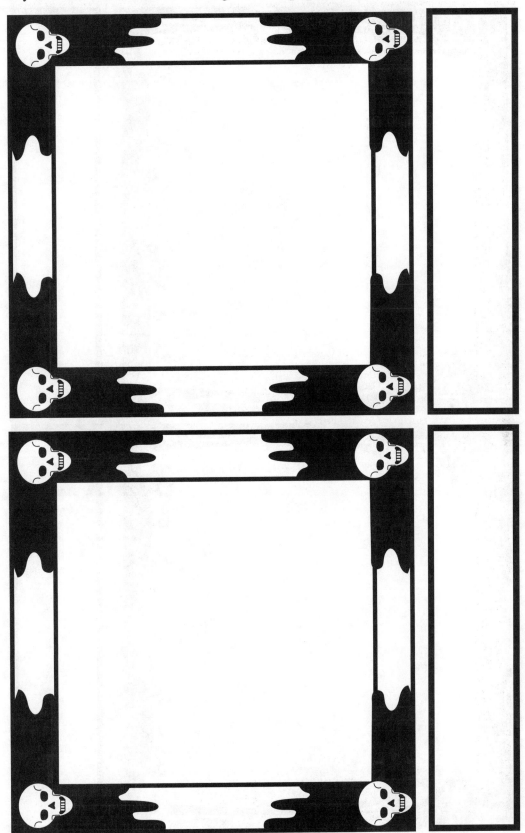

Trading Cards Template (cont.)

Create a master copy by copying the trading cards below twice and pasting four cards on one 8 ½" x 11" page. You may also mix and match the trading cards on pages 49–52.

Third-of-a-Page
Blank Bookmark Template

Reproduce this bookmark three times. Cut and paste to fill one sheet of paper.

Blank Postcard Template

Reproduce this postcard two times. Cut and paste to fill one sheet of paper.

"Today I Learned" Postcard Template

Reproduce this postcard two times. Cut and paste to fill one sheet of paper.

Today I learned. . . .

Door Exit Pass Template

Copy the Exit Pass twice. Cut and paste to fill one sheet of paper.

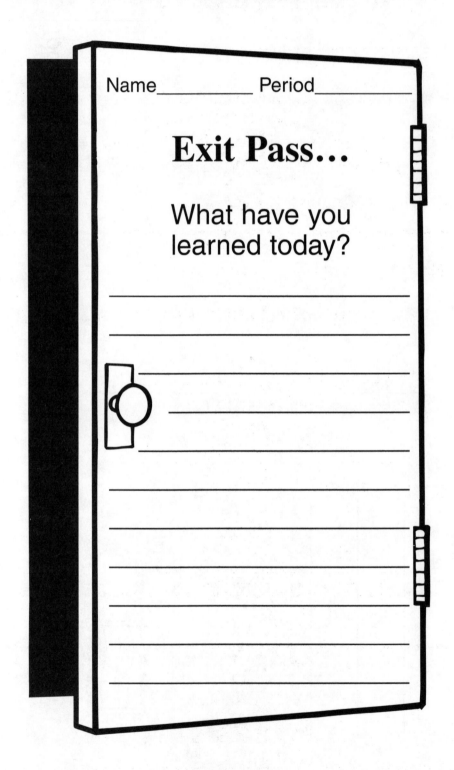

Name_____ Period_____

Exit Pass...

What have you learned today?

Gateway Exit Pass Template

Copy the Gateway Exit Pass twice. Cut and paste to fill one piece of paper.

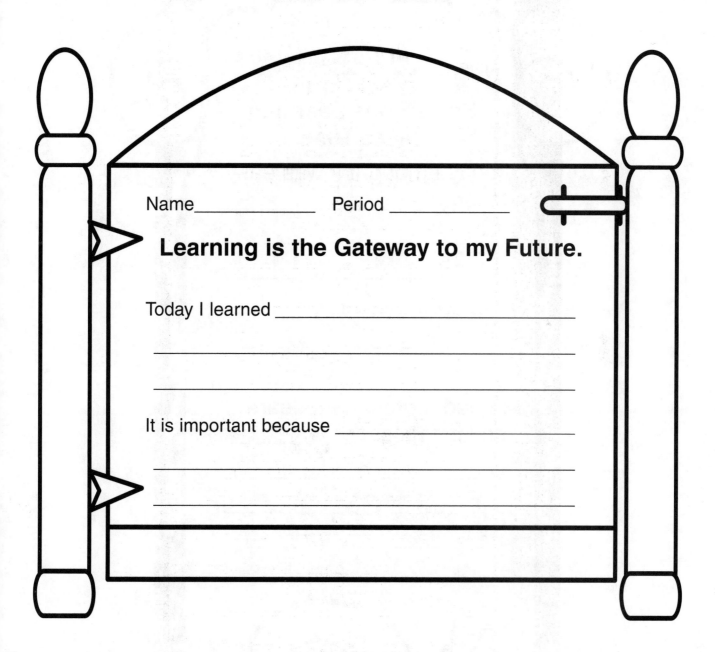

Name_____ Period _____

Learning is the Gateway to my Future.

Today I learned _____

_____

_____

It is important because _____

_____

_____

Snail Exit Pass Template

Copy the Snail Exit Pass twice. Cut and paste to fill one piece of paper.

Name: _____   Period: _____

Sometimes Learning Takes Time

Today I thought it was easy to learn…_____

_____

_____

_____

_____

I need more time to learn and practice… _____

_____

_____

_____

_____

58

Character Analysis Boxes Template

Copy the Character Analysis twice. Cut and paste to fill one sheet of paper. You can print on both sides of the paper so students can analyze two characters.

Name _____ Date _____

Character Analysis
Use the boxes below to record information
about your character.

Appearance	Actions
Thoughts/Feelings	Dialogue
Others' Reactions	Author's Direct Statements

"The Important Thing" Scaffold Template

Copy "The Important Thing" scaffold twice. Cut and paste to fill one sheet of paper.

Name _____ Date _____

"The Important Thing"

Topic

_____

The important thing about

_____

is that

_____

_____

_____

It is true that

_____

_____

But the important thing about

_____

is that

_____

_____

_____

60

Story Scaffold Template

Copy the Story Scaffold twice. Cut and paste to fill one sheet of paper. Students can use the reverse side to draw a picture about the story.

Name _____ Date _____

Story Scaffold

Title of Story _____

The Story begins when...

_____

_____

_____

The problem is…

_____

_____

The next thing that happened is…

_____

_____

Then…

_____

_____

After that…

_____

_____

The problem is solved when. . .

_____

_____

Textbook Frame Template

Copy the Textbook Frame twice. Cut and paste to fill one sheet of paper.

Name:_____ Date:_____

Question

_____

_____

Response:

1. Topic Sentence

_____

_____

2. Supporting Detail Sentence

_____

_____

3. Supporting Detail Sentence

_____

_____

4. Supporting Detail Sentence

_____

_____

_____

5. Summary/Conclusion Sentence

_____

_____

_____

Noun Picture and Sentences Student Instructions

Purpose: To write sentences using all the different types of nouns reviewed in class: common, proper, abstract, concrete, plural, and possessive.

Review

Write the definition and give examples for each type of noun:

1. Common Nouns

   Definition: _____

   Examples: _____

2. Proper Nouns

   Definition: _____

   Examples: _____

3. Abstract Nouns

   Definition: _____

   Examples: _____

4. Concrete Nouns

   Definition: _____

   Examples: _____

5. Plural Nouns:

   Definition: _____

   Examples: _____

6. Possessive Nouns:

   Definition: _____

   Examples: _____

Directions:

On a half sheet of paper, write one to two sentences that include all the different types of nouns. Important note: each noun falls into as least two different types.

Underline each noun in your sentence(s). Using a chart on the back, categorize each of your nouns.

Create a colorful picture to illustrate your sentence.

Adjective Picture and Sentences Student Instructions

Purpose: To write sentences using different types of adjectives: descriptive adjectives that show what kind, how many, and which one; a proper adjective; and either a comparative or superlative adjective.

Review

Write the definition and give examples of the following adjectives:

1. Descriptive Adjective—What Kind

    Definition: _____

    Examples: _____

2. Descriptive Adjective—How Many

    Definition: _____

    Examples: _____

3. Descriptive Adjective—Which One

    Definition: _____

    Examples: _____

4. Proper Adjective

    Definition: _____

    Examples: _____

5. Superlative and Comparative Adjectives

    Definition: _____

    Examples: _____

Directions for Adjective Picture and Sentences

1. On a half sheet of paper, write one to two sentences that include all the different types of adjectives. Important note: each adjective must modify a noun.

2. Underline each adjective in your sentence(s). On the back, list each adjective, tell what type it is, and what noun it modifies.

3. Create a colorful picture to illustrate your sentence(s).

Verb Picture and Sentences
Student Instructions

Purpose: To write sentences using a variety of verbs in their correct form.

Review

Remember that a verb shows action or state of being.

1. List five action verbs:

_____

_____

2. List three state of being verbs:

_____

_____

3. List the 23 helping verbs:

_____

_____

Directions for Verb Picture and Sentences

On a half sheet of paper, write a short paragraph that includes each of the following types of verbs:

- Three Action Verbs (Use three different ones.)
- Three Linking Verbs (Use three different ones.)
- Six Helping Verbs (Use six different ones.)

Underline each verb in your paragraph. Label each verb, and tell whether it is an action verb (AV), linking verb (LV), or helping verb (HV).

On the other side of the paper, create a colorful picture to illustrate your paragraph.

Sample Paragraph

As I <u>crept</u> into the forest, the smell of fire <u>was</u> in the air. If I <u>weren't</u> so afraid, I
  AV1   LV1   LV2

<u>would</u> <u>have</u> thought that I was <u>dreaming</u>. But the sound of animal cries filled the air, and I
HV1   HV2   AV3   AV4

<u>searched</u> for my father, who <u>had</u> entered the forest before me. He <u>must</u> have <u>been</u> able to
AV5   HV3   HV4   HV5

<u>smell</u> the fire. Where <u>could</u> he be? The situation <u>seemed</u> hopeless to me.
AV6   HV6   LV

Adverb Picture and Sentences Student Instructions

Purpose: To write sentences using a variety of adverbs in their correct form.

Review:

Remember that an adverb modifies a verb, an adjective, or another adverb. Adverbs tell where, when, how, or to what extent (how much or how long).

1. Make a list of at least 15 adverbs. _____

_____

Write a sentence for each type of adverb. Use a different adverb than the one used in the model.

2. Adverbs tell where: The forest fire started here.

_____

_____

3. Adverbs tell when: We promptly called the fire department.

_____

_____

4. Adverbs tell how: They carefully examined the scene.

_____

_____

5. Adverbs tell to what extent: He was quite proud of himself.

_____

_____

Directions for Adverb Picture and Sentences

On the bottom of a half sheet of paper, write one to two sentences that include each type of adverb.

Above what you have written, create a colorful picture to illustrate your sentence(s).

Underline each adverb in your sentence(s). On the back of the paper, list each adverb, tell the word it modifies, and tell what quality it shows (where, when, how, to what extent).

Preposition Strip Sentence
Student Instructions

Purpose: To write the world's longest sentence that includes as many prepositional phrases as you can.

Review of Prepositions

1. What is a preposition, and what does it do? _____

_____

_____

_____

2. List at least 15 different prepositions.

_____   _____   _____

_____   _____   _____

_____   _____   _____

_____   _____   _____

_____   _____   _____

Directions for preposition activity:

1. Using a long, half sheet of paper (5 ½" x 8 ½") write a sentence using as many different prepositional phrases as you can (at least 15). Each new prepositional phrase should start a new line. (Note: The sentence must have a subject and verb, too.)

2. At the beginning or end of each prepositional phrase, sketch what your object (or person) is doing in that prepositional phrase.

3. Underline each preposition used in your sentence.

Idiom Activity Student Instructions

On the front side of a half piece of paper, write out your idiom and colorfully illustrate the literal meaning of the phrase.   On the back, explain the real meaning.
Extra Credit: Find out where the expression originated.

1. bury the hatchet
2. grab the bull by the horns
3. a wolf in sheep's clothing
4. crying over spilled milk
5. rule of thumb
6. opening a can of worms
7. ace in the hole
8. putting the cart before the horse
9. There's light at the end of the tunnel.
10. wearing your heart on your sleeve
11. beyond a shadow of a doubt
12. silent as a clam
13. blowing your top
14. putting your foot in your mouth
15. stick in the mud
16. Don't count your chickens before they hatch.
17. behind the 8-ball
18. green thumb
19. making a mountain out of a molehill
20. hit the road
21. on the tip of my tongue
22. hit the nail on the head
23. raining cats and dogs
24. butterflies in my stomach
25. His bark is worse than his bite.
26. out of the frying pan and into the fire
27. bats in their belfry
28. Go fly a kite.
29. I'm all thumbs today.
30. letting the cat out of the bag
31. throw in the towel
32. pulling my leg
33. born with a silver spoon in her mouth
34. Now you're cooking with gas!
35. pot calling the kettle black
36. time flies

37. He's driving me up a wall.
38. She's going bananas.
39. Hold your horses.
40. I'm stuck on you.
41. on the fence
42. kicked the bucket
43. laughing his head off
44. Keep your shirt on.
45. Get off my case.
46. Does the cat have your tongue?
47. She flew the coop.
48. Don't beat around the bush.
49. Put on your thinking cap.
50. Go jump in the lake.
51. It's easy as pie.
52. He's on the ball.
53. She cried her eyes out.
54. Don't spill the beans.
55. ants in his pants
56. knocked his block off
57. at the end of your rope
58. Let your hair down.
59. Throw the baby out with the bath water.
60. He's all ears.
61. She's bent out of shape.
62. He's bull-headed.
63. by the skin of his teeth
64. She's a couch potato.
65. Don't be a chicken.
66. She's down in the dumps.
67. He's an eager beaver.
68. Use some elbow grease.
69. Give me a hand.
70. Hit the books.
71. Let sleeping dogs lie.
72. She's in over her head.

Type of Sentences Activity
Student Instructions

Purpose: To identify the four different types of sentences, and to practice using the four types through animal dialogue on a picture.

A. Define the four types of sentences (Remember, the type of punctuation helps identify which type):

    1. Declarative: _____

              _____

    2. Interrogative: _____

              _____

    3. Imperative: _____

              _____

    4. Exclamatory: _____

              _____

B. Look at your animal picture. In the space below, draft possible sentences the animal could be thinking or saying. Be creative.

    Declarative: _____

    _____

    Interrogative: _____

    _____

    Imperative: _____

    _____

    Exclamatory_____

    _____

C. Back your picture with a larger piece of white or colored paper (half a sheet), and write your final sentences on or around the picture. Make sure you identify the type of sentence in parenthesis.

Cap Flap Book Student Instructions

Purpose: To create a flap book that reviews the basic capitalization rules, including sentence examples demonstrating each rule.

Review

Write seven rules used for capitalization:

1. _____

2. _____

3. _____

4. _____

5. _____

6. _____

7. _____

Directions

A. To make flaps: Take four half sheets of paper and overlap so there is approximately one half inch between each sheet. (Diagram A). Fold top over until there are eight flaps showing. (Diagram B). On the top, staple to secure the fold.

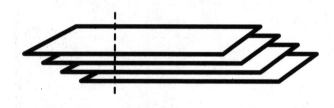

Diagram A

Diagram B

B. To add information: Put title, name, date, and period on top flap. On the remaining seven flaps, place a capitalization rule on the section that is showing. Lift flap above rule, and write at least two example sentences that demonstrate the capitalization rule. (Diagram C)

My birthday is in October.

We are going on vacation in July.

**Capitalize the names
of months**

Verb Comic Strip Student Instructions

Purpose: To practice using different types and forms of verbs by creating a comic strip about the actions of your favorite animal.

Directions

Divide (fold) a sheet of white paper into eighths. Number each section from 1–8. Each section needs to contain complete sentences, using the type of verbs identified, and a colorful drawing. (Note: All verbs must be underlined in each section.)

Section 1: Title of comic strip "What (name), My (animal), Can Do".

Section 2: Use a state of being verb.

Section 3: Use strong, vivid action verb(s).

Section 4: Use a helping verb with your main verb.

Section 5: Use the future tense form of a verb.

Section 6: Use the past participle of an irregular verb.

Section 7: Use one set of the "confusing" verbs.

Section 8: Write a question that uses a helping and main verb.

Example of Verb Comic Strip

Novel/Short Story Bookmark Template

(Part 1)

What is the main conflict in this story? Explain.

_____

_____

_____

_____

What kind of conflict is it? Explain. (Internal, external? Man vs. Man, Man vs. Society, Man vs. Self, Man vs. Nature?)

_____

_____

Plot Summary: Rising Action/Complications:

_____

_____

_____

_____

Climax

_____

_____

Falling Action/Resolution

_____

_____

_____

What is the Theme, or what are the Main Ideas of this story?

_____

Name _____

Place a picture of your author here...or draw a picture of a character or scene from your novel

_____
Author's Name
The Book I'm Reading is Titled:

_____

_____
This author has also written:

_____

_____
Exposition: Describe the Setting:

_____

_____

What inferences can you make from the title, the character's names, the format, the setting, or the first paragraph? (Can you guess what the story will be about from these?)

_____

_____

_____

Exposition: The Main Characters Are (give a short description of each)

_____

_____

_____

Novel/Short Story Bookmark Template

(Part 2)

Choose one quote (short passage) from the book and explain why you like it and what it means to you.

_____

_____

_____

_____

_____

_____

_____

_____

_____

_____

_____

_____

_____

_____

_____

_____

_____

Would you recommend this novel to another reader? Explain why or why not.

_____

_____

_____

_____

_____

_____

_____

_____

Vocabulary Building

Find 5 new words in the novel you are reading.

→ Copy down the sentence in which you find the word.

→ Underline the word.

→ Write the definition of the word in the blank below.

1. Your Word: _____

_____

Definition: _____

_____

_____

2. Your Word: _____

_____

Definition: _____

_____

_____

3. Your Word: _____

_____

Definition: _____

_____

_____

4. Your Word: _____

_____

Definition: _____

_____

_____

5. Your Word: _____

_____

Definition: _____

_____

Novel Review Bookmark Template

(Part 1)

Theme: the real meaning or message of the story. What lesson(s) did the character learn? What lesson(s) can be learned?

1. _____

   _____

   _____

   _____

   _____

   _____

2. _____

   _____

   _____

   _____

   _____

   _____

Quotes from the novel that reflect this theme:

1. _____

   _____

   _____

   _____

   _____

   _____

2. _____

   _____

   _____

   _____

   _____

So what? Why is this important?

1. _____

   _____

   _____

Name _____

Review a Novel Bookmark

Use this bookmark as you read to help you prepare for your essay.

Novel _____

Author _____

Analyze Literary Elements

Setting _____

_____

_____

Quote from novel that describes setting or its importance:

_____

_____

_____

_____

_____

_____

_____

_____

So what? How does the setting make a difference in the story?

_____

_____

_____

_____

Novel Review Bookmark Template

(Part 2)

Main Character(s)

_____

_____

_____

_____

_____

What does the author do to make the characters come alive?

_____

_____

_____

_____

How does the character deal with his struggles? What kind of person is he?

_____

_____

_____

_____

_____

Quote from the novel that shows the character's personality/traits:

_____

_____

So what? Why is this important to the story?

_____

_____

_____

_____

Plot: how does it help show the characters of the story?

_____

_____

_____

How does the author make the plot interesting?

_____

_____

_____

_____

_____

How does the plot help develop the theme of the story?

_____

_____

_____

_____

_____

So what? Why is this important to the story?

_____

_____

_____

_____

_____

_____

Would you recommend this novel? Why or why not?

_____

_____

_____

_____

_____

_____

_____

_____

_____

Vocabulary Poster Student Instructions

Purpose: To create a colorful poster that symbolically represents the meaning of a key vocabulary word, as well as include the definition, part of speech and use in a sentence.

Directions:

1. Write the teacher-assigned vocabulary word below:

   _____

2. Using a dictionary, write the appropriate definition:

   _____

3. What part of speech is the word?

   _____

4. Use the word in a sentence. (Make sure you demonstrate the meaning of the word through its use in the sentence.)

   _____

   _____

   _____

5. Using a sheet of white paper, draw a border that symbolically represents your word. (Be creative and colorful)

6. Recreate the word, using bubble, block, or logo-type lettering in large letters in the middle. Make sure the drawing of your word demonstrates part of the meaning.

7. In the remaining space above and below the word, include the definition, part of **speech** and the sentence your created using the word.

Example:

Vocabulary Square Template

Vocabulary Square

Name:_____
Period: _____
Date: _____

1.	3.
2.	4.

1.	3.
2.	4.

1.	3.
2.	4.

1.	3.
2.	4.

1. _____

2. _____

3. _____

4. _____

T-Notes Template

T-NOTES

Name:_____

Period: _____

Date: _____

Book Jacket Student Instructions

Purpose: To create a "book jacket" that tells about the book you have read, highlighting the story elements such as its setting, characters, conflicts, rising action events, and climax.

Instructions: There will be five panels. Each panel should be colorful, carefully drawn, and include detail. Be sure to include all the elements as described.

Folding Instructions for 8 ½" x 11" piece of paper: Measure across the 11" length, and make two marks, one at 4 ⅞", and the other at 5 ⅞". Fold the paper at these two places to create your book jacket. You may use larger paper if you desire.

Front of Page

Panel 1—Front Cover: Design a cover that includes the title, author's name, your name and period, and a detailed illustration. You may use original or computer art, but do not use the illustration on the cover of your book!

Panel 2—Spine: Use creative lettering to design a spine that includes the title of the book, author's name, and genre (mystery, fantasy, non-fiction, etc.)

Panel 3—Back Cover: Choose three problems that occurred, and draw a picture of each to illustrate it. Under each picture, state the problem using complete sentences. Then, beside the drawing, write a short paragraph using complete sentences describing the solution(s) to each problem.

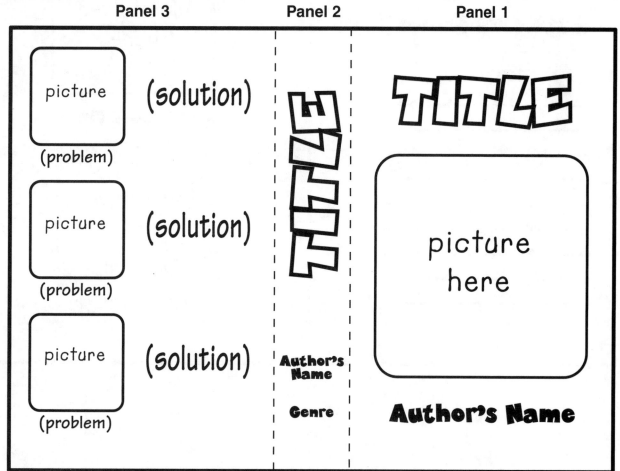

Book Jacket Student Instructions

Back of Page

Panel 4—Front Inside Panel: Include the book title, author and a detailed summary of the book that highlights the beginning, middle, and end of the story.

Panel 5—Back Inside Panel: Draw a picture of the main character and, using creative lettering, write the name of the character. Using the book and/or a thesaurus, find five adjectives that describe the character and explain how these words are relevant to the character. (Avoid using common, everyday words like nice, happy, pretty, etc.)

Panel 4   **Panel 5**

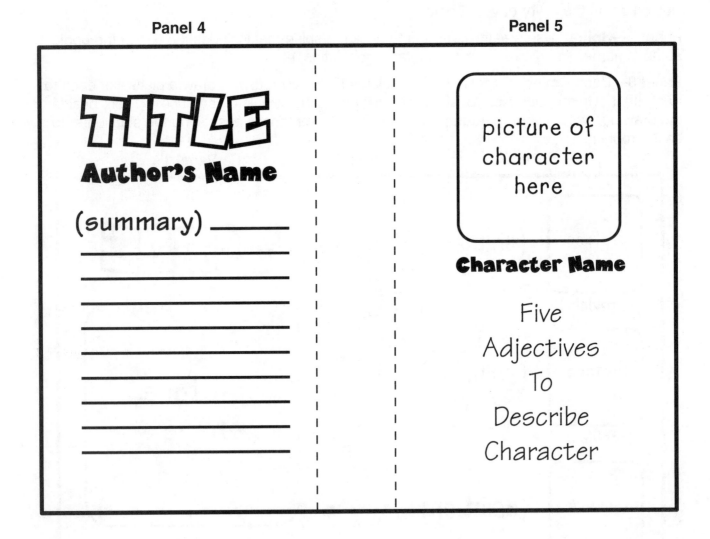